CONTENTS

INTRODUCTION AND SUMMARY

This document,[1] prepared by the staff of the Joint Committee on Taxation ("Joint Committee staff"), provides an analysis of the macroeconomic effects of a proposal to modify both the individual and corporate income tax by broadening their tax bases and changing statutory tax rates. This analysis is based on the proposal as it corresponds to the estimates presented in *Estimated Revenue Effects of the "Tax Reform Act of 2014"* (JCX-20-14), February 26, 2014 (and described in Discussion Draft CAMP_041).

The following analysis uses both an overlapping generations lifecycle model and the Joint Committee staff's Macroeconomic Equilibrium Growth model to simulate the macroeconomic effects of the proposal. In general, the lower effective marginal tax rates resulting from the combination of lower statutory tax rates and changes to the definition of taxable income provide an incentive for increased labor effort, and under some modeling assumptions for some years, increased business investment. Relative to present law, the policy provides an incentive for increased consumer purchases of goods and services by increasing after-tax income of households. This effect can be important when the economy is operating below full capacity. The extent of both supply and demand effects depends on the sensitivity of individual labor choices to changing effective marginal rates, the responsiveness of individual savings choices to changes in the after-tax return on earnings from investment, and the responsiveness of businesses to changing incentives for overall investment and the location of investment and taxable profits in the United States. In addition, the projected impacts of the proposal on the economy depend on assumptions about the monetary policy response by the Federal Reserve Board. In general, under most modeling assumptions, the proposal is projected to increase overall economic activity as measured by changes in gross domestic product ("GDP") relative to the present law baseline over the 10-year budget period.

---

[1] This document may be cited as follows: *Joint Committee on Taxation, Macroeconomic Analysis of the "Tax Reform Act of 2014,"* (JCX-22-13), February 26, 2014.

I. DESCRIPTION OF PROPOSAL

The following discussion analyzes the macroeconomic effects of a proposal to broaden the bases for the individual and corporate income tax and to restructure statutory tax rates on individual and corporate income. The proposal would be generally effective for taxable years beginning after December 31, 2014. This analysis is presented relative to the 2013 economic and receipts baseline ("present law"), published by the Congressional Budget Office ("CBO") in February, 2013.[2]

A. Individual Income Tax

Under present law, there are seven different regular individual income tax brackets, starting (in 2015 dollars) at 10 percent for single filers with taxable income under $9,200 and joint filers with taxable income under $18,400, and topping out at 39.6 percent for single filers with taxable income above $412,650 and joint filers with taxable income above $464,200. The proposal would reduce the number of tax brackets to two: single filers with taxable income below $37,400 and joint filers with taxable income below $74,800 would pay a top statutory tax rate of 10 percent while all other taxpayers would pay a statutory tax rate of 25 percent on taxable income above these amounts. Specific tax brackets are shown below in Table 1. The proposal slows the indexing of individual income tax brackets and other income thresholds by changing the index from the Consumer Price Index - for all urban consumers ("CPI-U") to the chained CPI. The proposal includes several other changes to tax rates on capital gains and dividends, phases out the 10 percent rate bracket and certain other deductions, eliminates the alternative minimum tax, and creates a surtax on certain income. Table 2 provides more detail about these changes.

Table 1.–Statutory Individual Income Tax Rates Under Present Law and Proposal

2015 Income Brackets for Single Filers (estimated)	2015 Income Brackets for Joint Filers (estimated)	Statutory Tax Rates (present law)	Statutory Tax Rates (proposal)
<$9,200	<$18,400	10	10
$9,200-$37,400	$18,401-$74,800	15	10
$37,401-$90,600	$74,801-$151,100	25	25
$90,601 - $189,000	$151,101-$230,100	28	25
$189,001-$410,950	$230,101-$410,950	33	25
$410,951-$412,650	$410,951-464,200	35	25
>$412,650	>$464,200	39.6	25

---

[2] Congressional Budget Office, *The Budget and Economic Outlook: Fiscal Years 2013-2023*, February 5, 2013.

The proposal also provides for a 10-percent surtax on certain sources of income as defined in a modified definition of adjusted gross income ("MAGI") above $400,000 for single filers and $450,000 for joint filers. In addition to the statutory rate changes, the proposal modifies or eliminates a number of individual income tax deductions, exclusions, and credits. The biggest changes include eliminating the deduction for State and local tax payments, reducing the principal cap associated with deductible home mortgage interest payments for new mortgages from $1 million to $500,000, reducing credit rates for the earned income credit, and converting certain excludable contributions to section 401(k) accounts into taxable contributions, with an exclusion at withdrawal. Other significant changes to the individual income tax base include an increase in the standard deduction but with a phase-out for filers with income above certain levels, repeal of the personal exemption, modification of credits for education expenses, and changes in allowable contributions to Roth Individual Retirement Arrangements.

Table 2.—Changes in Miscellaneous Statutory Tax Rates Between Present Law and the Proposal

Tax Rate Feature	Present Law	Proposal
Top tax rate on long term capital gains and qualified dividends	20%	Same as ordinary income rate, with 40% of gains and dividends excluded
Phase-out of the 10% statutory rate bracket.	No phase-out of the 10% statutory rate bracket	The 10% rate is phased out for single filers with income above $250,000 and joint filers with income above $300,000 (2013 dollars).
Phase-out of personal exemptions and itemized deductions	Personal exemptions and itemized deductions are phased out for single filers with income above $250,000 and joint filers with income above $300,000 (2013 dollars)	Personal exemptions are eliminated. The standard deduction or an equivalent amount of itemized deductions, followed by the child credit are phased out sequentially starting at the top of the phaseout range for the 10% rate bracket.
Surtax on modified AGI ("MAGI") where MAGI = AGI less charitable contributions and qualified domestic manufacturing income, plus various other sources of income excluded and expenses deducted from AGI under present law, including employer provided health benefits and the self-employed health deduction, 911 income, tax exempt interest, and untaxed social security benefits, and excluded 401(k) contributions	None	10% on modified AGI above $400,000 for single filers and $450,000 for joint filers
Alternative Minimum Tax	26% on alternative minimum taxable income below $175,000 (in 2012 dollars, indexed to inflation) and 28% on alternative minimum taxable income above that amount	None

B. Corporate Income Tax and Business-Related Provisions for Pass-Through Entities

Under present law, C corporations are taxed at a top statutory rate of 35 percent for corporations with taxable income over $10,000,000. C corporations with taxable income less than $50,000 are taxed at a rate of 15 percent; corporations with taxable income from $50,001-$75,000 are taxed at a rate of 25 percent, and C corporations with taxable income from $75,001 to $10,000,000 are taxed at a rate of 34 percent. The proposal would tax all C corporations at a rate of 25 percent, phased in at a two percentage point reduction from 2015 through 2019. Income of other business forms, including S corporations, partnerships and sole proprietorships, is taxed through the individual income tax code; thus the changes to statutory tax rates for the individual income tax under this proposal would also apply to the taxation of the business income of these pass-through entities.

Both the individual and corporate income tax frameworks include many different deductions, credits, and other special treatment of certain types of income and expenses of businesses. This proposal repeals or modifies a number of them. Some of the larger changes include eliminating the modified accelerated cost recovery system ("MACRS") and lengthening depreciable lives for depreciation of property placed in service after December 31, 2015, and requiring amortization instead of expensing of research and experimental expenditures and certain advertising expenses beginning in 2015. The repeal of MACRS is accompanied by indexing of depreciable basis to chained CPI-U. The proposal also repeals the 20-percent tax on minimum alternative taxable income of corporations.

C. Taxation of Multinational Corporations

The proposal also makes significant changes to the taxation of foreign income earned by U.S. multinational corporations. Under present law, the income of U.S. corporations is subject to U.S. corporate income tax whether it is earned within the U.S. or abroad, but a number of provisions reduce that liability. Such provisions include deferral of U.S. taxation of business income earned abroad by foreign subsidiaries until the income is repatriated; a credit against U.S. tax allowed for foreign income taxes paid; and current deductibility of expenses of U.S. parent companies, such as interest that supports foreign income on which U.S. tax is deferred. Many U.S. multinational corporations reduce their overall tax liability significantly relative to the amount of tax they would pay under a worldwide corporate income tax system in which they would pay U.S. tax on all their income, domestic and foreign, when earned. The proposal broadly replaces the current system with a 95-percent exemption for dividends received by U.S. corporations from foreign subsidiaries attributable to foreign business income of those subsidiaries.

Present law includes rules (commonly referred to as subpart F) to tax certain items of passive or mobile foreign subsidiary income when that income is earned rather than when it is repatriated. The proposal substantially modifies the subpart F rules, chiefly by providing broad taxation of all intangible income of foreign subsidiaries when the income is earned, with intangible income from serving foreign markets taxed at a reduced rate of 15 percent once the proposal is fully phased in. The proposal provides the same reduced rate of tax on foreign intangible income of U.S. parent companies. The proposal includes a one-time transition tax, subject to a foreign tax credit, on all previously untaxed foreign earnings and profits of foreign subsidiaries of U.S. corporations. The proposal also includes thin capitalization rules that restrict the deduction for interest expense of U.S. parent companies when, among other requirements, the U.S. members of the worldwide group are more heavily leveraged than the overall group. The net effect of the proposed changes to taxation of U.S. multinational corporations is to increase their U.S. income tax liability.

D. Conventional Estimate of the Effects of the Proposal

Under our conventional revenue estimating methodology, this proposal is projected to result in an increase in revenues of about $3 billion over the 2014-2023 budget period relative to present law. The proposal is projected to result in a reduction in individual income tax payments (not including revenues due to broadening the taxable base of pass-through businesses) of about $590 billion over that budget period. The year-by-year conventional revenue estimate for this proposal relative to current policy appears in *Estimated Revenue Effects of the "Tax Reform Act of 2014,"* (JCX-20-14).

II. MODELING APPROACHES AND MACROECONOMIC ANALYSIS

The following analysis was performed using the Joint Committee on Taxation staff's Macroeconomic Equilibrium Growth model ("MEG")[3] and an overlapping generations lifecycle model ("OLG").[4] Information about parameter assumptions that are key to determining behavioral responses in each model appear in the Appendix. Both models start with the standard, neoclassical assumption that the amount of output is determined by the availability of labor and capital, and in the long run aggregate demand equals aggregate supply. Individuals are assumed to make decisions based on observed characteristics of the economy, including wages, prices, interest rates, tax rates, and government spending levels.

In the MEG model, monetary policy conducted by the Federal Reserve Board is explicitly modeled, with lagged price adjustments allowing for the economy to be temporarily out of equilibrium in response to fiscal and monetary policy changes. Labor supply decisions are modeled separately for four groups: low income primary earners, low income secondary earners, other primary earners, and other secondary earners. Firms make investment decisions based on an expected after-tax rate of return. Individuals in the MEG model do not anticipate future changes in the economy or government finances; thus, this type of model is often referred to as a "myopic" behavior model. This feature of the MEG model allows the simulation of tax and government expenditure policy that may result in an unsustainable growth path. Specifically, policies that result in the Federal debt increasing or decreasing at a faster rate than the growth of GDP can be modeled.

In the OLG model, individuals are assumed to make consumption and labor supply decisions in order to maximize their lifetime well-being given the resources they can foresee will be available to them. They are assumed to have complete information, or "perfect foresight," about economic conditions, such as wages, prices, interest rates, tax rates, and government spending, over their lifetimes. Economic decisions are modeled separately for each of 55 adult-age cohorts. Firms' investment decisions respond to the effects of tax policy on the expected future value of the firm. Changes in marginal tax rates on firm profits, and changes in the value of deductions for investment affect this future valuation. The version of OLG used in this analysis includes a separate multinational corporation ("MNC") sector that uses both capital and intellectual property in the production of goods and services.

We analyze the proposal using varying assumptions about several types of taxpayer and Federal Reserve Board response to the proposed tax changes. We rely on information from

---

[3] A detailed description of the MEG model and its behavioral parameters may be found in: Joint Committee on Taxation, *Macroeconomic Analysis of Various Proposals to Provide $500 Billion in Tax Relief,* (JCX-4-05), March 1, 2005, and Joint Committee on Taxation, *Overview of the Work of the Staff of the Joint Committee on Taxation to Model the Macroeconomic Effects of Proposed Tax Legislation to Comply with House Rule XIII.3(h)(2)*, (JCX-105-03), December 22, 2003.

[4] The OLG model used in this analysis was leased from Tax Policy Advisers. Information about this model may be found in John W. Diamond and George R. Zodrow, *Description of the Tax Policy Advisers Model,* unpublished document, 2013.

various JCT tax models[5] used in the production of conventional revenue estimates to obtain information about the effects of the proposal on individual and business average and effective marginal tax rates, and on after-tax returns to capital and labor to characterize the tax proposal within the MEG and OLG models. Changes in both statutory tax rates and the definition of taxable income can impact effective marginal tax rates as well as average tax rates.

The MEG model is used to examine the importance of different assumptions about Federal Reserve policy. Under the "Aggressive Fed" policy, it is assumed that the Federal Reserve Board would work to counteract any demand incentives resulting from fiscal policy. For this proposal, since the policy results in a net decrease in income tax paid by individuals, providing them with more take home income for consumption purposes, the aggressive Fed simulation would include an immediate increase in interest rates to counteract these demand effects. The "Neutral Fed" simulations assume that the Federal Reserve Board targets a fixed monetary growth rate, and does not try to counteract fiscal policy.

The MEG model is also used to present results using differing assumptions about the responsiveness of labor to changes in effective marginal tax rates and average taxes for each proposal. The "High Labor Elasticity" simulations use labor supply responsiveness parameters that are consistent with the upper range of measured response levels from empirical studies. The "Low Labor Elasticity" simulations reduce the responsiveness to changes in effective marginal tax rates by 50 percent.

Both the MEG and OLG models are used to explore the impact of varying assumptions about the responsiveness of capital investment and international capital flows to tax policy changes. In the MEG model, there is no explicit distinction between domestic and multinational corporations. International capital flows respond to changes in the after-tax rate of return on capital between the United States and the rest of the world, as well as to changes in the relative attractiveness of imports and exports. In contrast, the OLG model has several different types of businesses, including a multinational corporate ("MNC") sector with foreign subsidiaries. The addition of foreign subsidiaries presents the MNC with the ability to optimize over both the location of investments (both highly mobile intellectual property ("IP") and capital), as well as some ability to shift profits from the U.S. parent to low tax subsidiaries. The ability of MNC to shift profits from the United States to low tax jurisdictions is meant to capture the many ways that firms can shift their profit overseas, including transfer pricing, debt leveraging, interest stripping, and hybrid instruments. The OLG model treats all of these different types of profit shifting strategies the same and limits the amount of shifting to the extra-normal returns to IP.[6]

---

[5] Descriptions of the JCT conventional estimating models may be found in JCX-46-11, *Testimony of the Staff of the Joint Committee on Taxation before the House Committee on Ways and Means Regarding Economic Modeling*, September 21, 2011 and other documents at www.jct.gov under "Estimating Methodology."

[6] The MNC modeling follows the work in M.P. Devereux and R. de Mooij in "An applied analysis of ACE and CBIT reforms in the EU," *International Tax and Public Finance*, 18(1), 2011, 93-120 and M.P. Devereux, L. Bettendorf, A. van der Horst, S. Loretz. And R. de Mooij, "Corporate tax harmonization in the EU," *Economic Policy*, 63, 2010, 537-590.

This analysis presents two OLG simulations that vary the degree of responsiveness of this MNC sector to changes in tax policy. In particular, we vary the responsiveness of MNCs to shifting intellectual property and profits. The "default IP elasticities" simulation reflects the calibration of the model to hit estimates for cross-border capital movements under present law, with the relatively mobile intellectual property estimated to be roughly 8.5 times more responsive than capital. Profit shifting is calibrated to be about 20 percent of the corporate tax base in 2013, consistent with the middle point of estimates of this shifting under present law. We present an additional simulation ("reduced IP elasticities") in which the IP responsiveness is assumed to be the same as that of capital, and the profit shifting elasticity is reduced by about one third.

One important difference between the MEG and OLG models is in their treatment of Federal fiscal policy. In the MEG model, it is possible to simulate structural Federal budget deficits as forecast in the CBO baseline and to allow for increases or decreases in the deficit in simulating proposals. In contrast, the OLG model cannot simulate either the present law fiscal baseline or policy proposals that incorporate unsustainable Federal budget deficits or surpluses. The MEG model assumes individuals cannot foresee future unsustainable Federal budget conditions, while the OLG model assumes that individuals have perfect foresight about the economy, including unsustainable Federal budget conditions. Thus, in the OLG model there is no equilibrium solution when Federal budget conditions appear unsustainable in the long run. It is necessary to create counterfactual stable ratios of debt to GDP within both the baseline and policy simulations of the OLG model.

Because both present-law fiscal conditions and the path of the budget deficit are necessarily modeled differently within the OLG and MEG models, it is difficult to compare the results between the two models directly, as they are essentially modeling different types of economies. Because the MEG model simulates the effects of the actual proposed law, its results are of interest. Because the MEG model assumes people are unable to foresee the probable effects of the proposed law change, while the OLG model assumes that people can foresee these effects, the OLG model provides a useful alternative perspective on the economy.

The OLG simulations presented here include an assumption in the base (present law) simulation that average tax rates are higher and transfer payments are lower than they actually are. To the extent that the policy simulation changes the path of debt growth, it is necessary to include a fiscal policy reaction function so that the debt to GDP ratio does not change significantly in the policy simulation. The specific changes in tax and spending that are used to provide fiscal balance can affect results. Because this proposal results in increased economic growth and decreasing deficits, the fiscal balance reaction to the policy requires either an increase in government outlays or a decrease in taxes. These simulations adjust transfer payments, thereby allowing us to analyze the specific tax policy in the proposal.

Following is a series of tables that show the effects of this proposal on real (inflation adjusted) gross domestic product, business capital stock, employment, and consumption. Results from each policy simulation for each variable are presented as percentage changes from the present-law baseline forecast values for the variables in each of Tables 3-7 below. The Joint Committee staff configures the present-law baseline forecasts for Federal government receipts and spending in the MEG model to approximate the February 2013 forecast of the CBO[7] as closely as possible.

---

[7] Congressional Budget Office, *The Budget and Economic Outlook: Fiscal Years 2013-2023*, February 5, 2013.

III. EFFECTS ON ECONOMIC ACTIVITY AND REVENUES

A. Effects on Real Gross Domestic Product and Revenues

In the MEG model, economic growth responds to changes in average and effective marginal tax rates on labor, and changes in the after-tax return to capital. In the OLG model, economic growth also responds to changes in average and effective marginal tax rates on labor, as well as to changes in the anticipated after-tax value of firms. Changes in tax rates on interest, dividends, and capital gains income, as well as on business profits accruing to corporations and pass-through entities, affect the after-tax return to capital and the anticipated after-tax value of firms.

The level of economic activity also responds to changes in the after-tax income of individuals under certain assumptions about the current state of the baseline economy and Federal Reserve policy. During periods when the economy is operating below its full employment capacity - when not all available labor or capital is employed - increases in after-tax income increase demand for goods and services, leading to more economic growth.

This proposal reduces the overall effective marginal tax rate on labor, providing an incentive for people to work, supplying more labor to the economy. The importance of this effect depends on how responsive labor is to these changes. The proposal also increases the after-tax income of individuals by reducing individual tax rates overall, thus increasing demand for goods and services. Because the economy is currently operating below full employment levels, this increased demand can be expected to lead to an increase in economic output, to the extent that Federal Reserve policy does not take action to counteract this effect.

The proposal reduces effective marginal tax rates on interest and rental income and business profits of corporations and pass-through entities relative to present law, which increases the after-tax return to capital. But it also reduces a number of credits and deductions, the largest of which are inventory and depreciation deductions, which reduces the after-tax return to capital relative to present law. On net, the after-tax return to business capital is reduced relative to present law by these changes overall.

The proposal is projected to result in increases in economic activity relative to that projected under present law, as measured by changes in real GDP. The increase in projected economic activity is projected to increase revenues relative to the conventional revenue estimate by $50 to $700 billion, depending on which modeling assumptions are used, over the 10-year budget period.

Table 3.–Percent Change in Real GDP Relative to Present Law

		Fiscal years 2014-2018	Fiscal Years 2019-2023	Fiscal Years 2014-2023
MEG				
High labor elasticity	Aggressive Fed	0.2%	0.2%	0.2%
	Neutral Fed	0.1%	0.8%	0.5%
Low Labor Elasticity	Aggressive Fed	0.2%	0.1%	0.1%
	Neutral Fed	0.1%	0.7%	0.4%
MEG, reduced investment response to taxation of multinationals				
High labor elasticity	Aggressive Fed	0.3%	0.3%	0.3%
	Neutral Fed	0.3%	0.8%	0.6%
OLG				
Default IP elasticities		1.8%	1.4%	1.5%
Reduced IP elasticities		1.8%	1.4%	1.6%

Table 3 (above) shows the predicted effects of this policy on real gross domestic product, relative to what is projected under present law for the proposal. These changes are shown for the first five years, second five years, and full 10 years of the standard budget window. GDP is projected to grow by 0.1 percent to 1.6 percent during the 10-year budget period. The positive growth effects of the proposal arise primarily from its effects on labor supply and consumption demand. In the following sections on capital stock, employment, and consumption effects, the influence of the proposal on each of these components of growth and the economy can be seen in more detail.

In the standard MEG model simulations, the larger growth effects occur in simulations that assume more labor response to reductions in effective marginal tax rates, and in which the Federal Reserve Board is assumed not to moderate increases in demand arising from higher after-tax income.

An additional modeling assumption affecting the projected effects of this proposal is the extent to which changes in the taxation of foreign income and income from intellectual property are expected to provide an incentive for more investment and profit reporting within the United States. The MEG model is not designed to model specifically the difference between IP and capital or the effects of shifting of reported profits between countries to take advantage of differences in relative tax rates. The conventional revenue estimate accounts for the effects of the latter behavior on revenues, but not on economic activity. In the OLG model, the ability to shift profits to minimize tax liability without shifting economic activity results in increased economic activity within the United States. To approximate the separate modeling of these effects using the MEG model, we assume that the various tax increasing portions of the changes on taxation of multinational corporations and intellectual property do not affect their investment incentives, as shown in the "MEG, reduced investment response to taxation of multinationals" simulations. In these simulations, anticipated GDP growth is higher than in the base MEG simulations.

B. Effects on the Capital Stock

The reduction in statutory tax rates on corporate and non-corporate business income increases the after-tax return to investment for some businesses that do not make use of many of the business deductions under present law. For those businesses that do make use of accelerated depreciation, expensing of research and experimentation expenses, or other business tax expenditures, the elimination of these provisions is expected to reduce the after-tax return on investment. Overall, the proposal is expected to increase the cost of capital for domestic firms, thus reducing the incentive for investment in domestic capital stock.

Table 4 shows the expected change in business capital relative to what was projected to occur under the present law baseline, but does not indicate a reduction in capital stock over time. In other words, the negative numbers in these tables result from a projected slower rate of growth in capital due to the proposal. Investment in capital is generally projected to increase slightly relative to present law in the first half of the budget period, and decrease relative to present law in the second half. The repeal of accelerated depreciation does not occur until 2016, thus delaying the negative influence of this provision, at the same time that reduced tax rates on income from capital are providing an incentive for increased investment. Over time, the cumulative effects of the repeal of MACRS and amortization of intellectual property begin to outweigh the positive incentives from reduced rates in standard MEG simulations.

As mentioned above, a crucial modeling assumption for analyzing this proposal is predicting the extent to which the changes in the taxation of foreign capital will provide an incentive for both U.S. multinational and foreign corporations to shift investment and profits to the United States. Because the proposal treats domestic investment in intellectual property less favorably and earnings on some foreign income more favorably than under present law, in the simulations with reduced sensitivity of the location of intellectual property to changes in taxation, the effects of reducing responsiveness to incentives for foreign-based capital investment, particularly in intellectual property, are shown to reverse or dampen (depending on the degree of responsiveness assumed) the negative effects on capital stock generated by the increased cost of domestic capital.

Table 4.–Percent Change in Business Capital Relative to Present Law

		Fiscal years 2014-2018	Fiscal Years 2019-2023	Fiscal Years 2014-2023
MEG				
High labor elasticity	Aggressive Fed	0.1%	-1.0%	-0.5%
	Neutral Fed	0.0%	-0.5%	-0.3%
Low labor elasticity	Aggressive Fed	0.1%	-1.0%	-0.6%
	Neutral Fed	0.0%	-0.6%	-0.3%
MEG, reduced investment response to taxation of multinationals				
High labor elasticity	Aggressive Fed	0.3%	-0.6%	-0.2%
	Neutral Fed	0.2%	-0.2%	0.0%
OLG				
Default IP elasticities		0.2%	0.0%	0.1%
Reduced IP elasticities		0.0%	-0.3%	-0.2%

C. Effects on Private Sector Employment

Reductions in effective marginal tax rates on labor - that is, increases in the portion of wages from additional work effort that a person keeps - provide an incentive for people to work more, supplying more labor to the economy. Somewhat offsetting that effect, reductions in total individual tax payments (as measured by changes in the average tax rate), increase peoples' total take home income, providing an incentive for people to work less. Policies that reduce effective marginal tax rates by more than average tax rates generally provide a net incentive for more labor to be supplied by the economy. This proposal reduces effective marginal and average tax rates on labor overall relative to present law. Table 5 below shows the predicted effects of these changes on peoples' willingness to work. As a result of this proposal, labor force participation is projected to increase relative to present law from 0.3 percent to 1.5 percent over the 10-year budget period. In the MEG model, labor force participation is affected by assumed labor force responsiveness parameters. Labor force response is higher in the OLG simulations than in the MEG simulations in part because the capital stock declines less in the OLG simulations, thus allowing for relatively less reduction or more increase in labor productivity and wages. In addition, labor is more responsive in the OLG model than in the MEG model.

Table 5.–Percent Change in Labor Force Participation Relative to Present Law

		Fiscal years 2014-2018	Fiscal Years 2019-2023	Fiscal Years 2014-2023
MEG				
High labor elasticity	Aggressive Fed	0.3%	0.4%	0.3%
	Neutral Fed	0.3%	0.4%	0.3%
Low labor elasticity	Aggressive Fed	0.2%	0.3%	0.3%
	Neutral Fed	0.2%	0.3%	0.3%
MEG, reduced investment response to taxation of multinational				
High labor elasticity	Aggressive Fed	0.3%	0.4%	0.3%
	Neutral Fed	0.3%	0.4%	0.3%
OLG				
Default IP elasticities		1.4%	1.3%	1.3%
Reduced IP elasticities		1.5%	1.5%	1.5%

17

Table 6 shows changes in employment predicted to result from the proposal. While the willingness of people to work at a given combination of wage rates and taxes on wages is an important component of total employment, changes in employment are also influenced by the amount of business demand for labor. Relative to present law, the proposal results in a net increase in after-tax income, leading consumers to demand more goods and services, and employers to increase output. Because the proposal reduces the after-tax return to capital relative to present law, businesses are expected to substitute some labor for capital. In some MEG simulations, employment is projected to increase by somewhat more than the labor force as a result of this increased demand for labor services, thereby reducing unemployment. As expected, the projected increase in labor force is more sensitive to assumptions about the elasticity of labor to marginal tax rates, while the projected increase in employment is also quite sensitive to actions of the Federal Reserve Board. In the OLG simulations, it is assumed there is no involuntary unemployment, and thus changes in employment are the same as changes in the labor force.

Table 6.–Percent Change in Private Sector Employment Relative to Present Law

		Fiscal years 2014-2018	Fiscal Years 2019-2023	Fiscal Years 2014-2023
MEG				
High labor elasticity	Aggressive Fed	0.3%	0.6%	0.5%
	Neutral Fed	0.2%	1.3%	0.7%
Low labor elasticity	Aggressive Fed	0.3%	0.5%	0.4%
	Neutral Fed	0.2%	1.2%	0.7%
MEG, reduced investment response to taxation of multinationals				
High labor elasticity	Aggressive Fed	0.4%	0.6%	0.5%
	Neutral Fed	0.4%	1.2%	0.8%
OLG				
Default IP elasticities		1.4%	1.3%	1.3%
Reduced IP elasticities		1.5%	1.5%	1.5%

D. Effects on Consumption

Table 7 shows how the proposal affects consumption relative to present law. In addition to the interaction between consumption demand and short-term economic growth, consumption is often of interest as an indicator of individuals' well-being. Generally, increased growth and employment facilitate more consumption, with consumption increasing relative to present law by between 0.4 percent and 2.1 percent over the 10-year budget window. The increased labor supply due to reduced marginal rates, and increase in after-tax income relative to present law allow for a substantial increase in consumption, consistent with the increasing pressures on demand described above. Consumption is also increased because the slightly reduced after-tax return to capital reduces incentives to save. Those simulations that predict higher employment generally also predict higher consumption.

Table 7.—Percent Change in Consumption Relative to Present Law
(base proposal)

		Fiscal years 2014-2018	Fiscal Years 2019-2023	Fiscal Years 2014-2023
MEG				
High labor elasticity	Aggressive Fed	0.3%	0.6%	0.5%
	Neutral Fed	0.2%	1.1%	0.7%
Low labor elasticity	Aggressive Fed	0.2%	0.6%	0.4%
	Neutral Fed	0.1%	1.0%	0.6%
MEG, reduced investment response to taxation of multinationals				
High labor elasticity	Aggressive Fed	0.2%	0.7%	0.5%
	Neutral Fed	0.2%	1.1%	0.7%
OLG				
Default IP elasticities		2.3%	1.9%	2.1%
Reduced IP elasticities		2.2%	1.9%	2.0%

E. Conclusion

Broadening of the individual and corporate income tax bases through elimination of many preferences in the form of deductions, exemptions, and tax credits allows for a reduction in average and effective marginal tax rates for most individual taxpayers, which provides both an incentive for increased labor effort, and an increase in demand for goods and services. These changes also reduce the after-tax return to investment under many modeling assumptions, providing an incentive for a reduction in the U.S. domestic capital stock. On net, these changes are expected to result in an increase in economic output relative to present law.

APPENDIX - KEY PARAMETER ASSUMPTIONS

The amount of taxpayer response to changes in fiscal policy is governed by how sensitive their work, consumption and savings decisions are to changes in their disposable income, and to changes in the after-tax rate of return to additional work or investment. Tables A-1 and A-2 below show the parameters used to model the degree of responsiveness for the MEG and OLG models respectively.

Table A.1- Key Parameter Assumptions in the MEG Model

Labor supply elasticities in disaggregated labor supply	Income	High Elasticity Substitution	Low Elasticity Substitution
Low income primary	-0.1	0.2	0.15
Other primary	-0.1	0.1	0.1
Low income secondary	-0.3	0.8	0.4
Other secondary	-0.2	0.6	0.3
Wage-weighted population average with baseline rates	-0.1	0.2	0.1
Savings/consumption parameters			
Rate of time preference	0.015		
Intertemporal elasticity of substitution	0.35		
Derived long-run savings elasticity to the after-tax rate of return on capital	0.25		

Table A.2 Key Parameter Assumptions in the OLG Model

Description	Value
Time preference	0.015
Intertemporal elasticity of substitution	0.4
Intratemporal elasticity of substitution between	
consumption and leisure	0.6
Leisure share of time endowment	0.4
Population growth rate	0.015
Technological growth rate	0.019
Capital share for	
Corporate	0.2
Multinational (not including IP)	0.15
Non-corporate	0.3
Housing	0.985
Adjustment cost*	5.0
Debt-to-capital ratio (average)	0.35
Substitution elasticity between capital and labor in	
Non-housing†	1.0
Housing†	1.0
Substitution elasticity for intellectual property‡	
Default elasticity	8.6
Low elasticity	1.0

*Quadratic adjustment cost function

†Cobb-Douglas production function

‡Substitution elasticity between foreign and domestic after-tax profits
    attributable to intellectual property